KINGSWOOD

1. Two Mile Hill looking towards Kingswood, at the junction with New Queen Street and Kingsway. This view was taken about 1938, and shows a tram about to enter the single track section towards St. George.

2. A close-up view of tram 187 taken about the same time in 1938. Just above the junction with New Queen Street.

3. Members of the Zion Methodist Chapel taking part in the annual Whitsun parade in 1914. This view is of the same area of Two Mile Hill at the corner with New Queen Street.

4. Looking in the opposite direction, with the Band of Hope band, connected with the Evangelist Sunday School, showing their banner, what a great event the Whitsun Parades were, and still are today.

ZION CHAPEL, REGENT STREET, KINGSWOOD.

5. The Zion Chapel on the corner of Grantham Road, a Chapel much associated with music. Samuel Burchell, for many years their music master, entered their choir for the first Bristol Music Festival in 1873. He organised many concerts at the Chapel in aid of the poor.

6. Regent Street looking towards the Clock Tower, a group of boys awaiting the unloading of the Evening World. This paper, first published in 1932, finally closed in 1962.

7. Regent Street at the corner with Downend Road, the turning behind the hand-cart. This postcard view, posted December 24th 1907, dates from before the two end houses on the right were removed, and the houses opposite converted to shops.

8. The Picture House in Regent Street, the entrance being somewhat dwarfed by the garage and engineering works next door. The Ambassador Cinema, with a much larger capacity opened in 1938 adjoining Dr. Grace's Surgery. The Cinema was later renamed the Odeon.

REGENT STREET, KINGSWOOD. (No. 2.)   PUBLISHED BY C. W. SHIPP, KINGSWOOD BRISTOL.

9. Regent Street looking in the direction of St. George, with the Midland Railway Parcels and Receiving Office in the same premises as the newsagent. This postcard was published locally by C.W. Shipp and posted on July 17th 1907.

10. Regent Street. This 1950s view with cottages, the Odeon Cinema, and Dr. Grace's Surgery, as it was before being pulled down to make way for the later building of Kings Chase Shopping Centre.

11. Regent Street with the busy shopping centre. The building with the Pinnacle (on the right) built in 1892, is on the corner with Moravian Road.

12. Looking in the opposite direction, showing the variation in architecture, and the tram lines now in two lanes. Many trade names famous about World War II and after about such as Pearkes Store and Hodders the Chemist.

13. Regent Street about 1953. Dr. Grace's Surgery in the distance.

14. Regent Street, a closer view of Dr. Grace's, with the Clock Tower beyond. This postcard is in the same series as illustration number 13, published in 1953. A British Railways lorry is making a delivery on the right, in the early years after the change from the G.W.R.

15. The Jubilee Memorial clock, erected to commemorate Queen Victoria's Diamond Jubilee in 1897, and opposite the early shop and cottages. On the end wall of the shops further along the road is an advertisement for Jones Patent Flour.

16. Opposite the Jubilee Clock, new shops were built, including J.H. Mills, Grocer. This summer view in about 1918. Note the interesting ornate ironwork above the shop blinds.

17. Regent Street at the junction with Hanham Road. (In this picture the publishers have named it High Street). The Kingswood Hotel is on the corner. This postcard was published by Hepworth in the 1920s.

18. Taken in the opposite direction to illustration number 17, but a few years earlier, about 1917, showing the round turret design of Lloyds Bank, with tram 178 approaching the terminus from Old Market.

19. The Park. A turning off of Park Road in 1922, with tennis courts in a delightful rural setting. The road is now much widened with modern houses built.

20. The Park, showing a few of the houses built by Alfred James Bridges. He intended to build a circle of houses, but went bankrupt before they could be completed.

21. Mr. A.J. Bridges' son owned the local brickworks. He is the rider of this Scott two stroke water cooled motorbike built in 1911, with a Bath number plate. This picture was taken in The Park.

22. Dot Cowley, a famous lady Speedway rider in her day. This picture was taken in 1928 and she is seen here in her motor cycle gear on a Douglas motorbike built in Kingswood.

23. Budgets Private Park, which is now known as The Park, showing a few houses built by Alfred James Bridges, which are now surrounded by the modern houses of today.

24. St. Joseph's, the first corrugated iron church and monastery, situated in Park Road opposite British Schoolroom. St. Joseph's church is now re-built in Lodge Causeway, Fishponds. This postcard was postally used in April 1909.

25. A Whitsuntide Parade taken by Plucknett of Kingswood, the first girl in the parade is Mr. Plucknett's daughter. She later married Graham Bamford, a member of a well-known Kingswood family. This postcard was posted in 1929.

26. The "Made for Ever" Wesleyan Sunday School Parade with decorated float, at the corner of Anchor Road and Fisher Road. They are about to join the Whitsuntide procession in the early 1920s.

27. The Whitsuntide Parade, an annual event of witness for the local churches in the Kingswood area. This float by the Band of Hope is passing E. Jefferies shop in Two Mile Hill.

28. The Boys Brigade with their band taking part in the procession for the annual Whitsun event. This picture, taken by Plucknett, shows them passing the awning of the shop of A. Wiltshire, Boot Stores.

29. Arthur Caddick, sign writer, poster and ticket writer outside his shop at 31 Regent Street. Standing with him is Ella Caddick and one of their apprentices. Arthur entered the business at the age of fifteen.

30. The workroom above Arthur Caddick's shop, with staff working on orders. The maps on the wall no doubt helped with delivery locations.

31. Arthur Caddick's business designed the mannequins and art work for Unity Corsetry, which had a factory in Kingswood. Arthur is seen working on the left with two of his staff.

32. One of the many window displays advertising the range of Unity Corsetry, using Arthur Caddick's designs and mannequins.

33. The Kingswood Bulb and Corn Stores next door to Arthur Caddicks, opposite Blackhorse Road. The adjoining shop was owned by F.E. Knott, who sold general goods and ironmongery.

34. This back view of Whitefield's Old Tabernacle in Park Road, shows the School Room and Graveyard, from the Caretakers House.

35. Bright Street with the single bay terraced houses, before 1910. The street connects between Moravian Road and Hanham Road.

36. Laurel Street runs parallel with Bright Street, connecting with the same two roads, and through to Derrick Street across Moravian Road. Pictured again before 1910 and taken by the same photographer as illustration 35.

37. An aerial view of Kingswood taken from the Church Tower, with High Street in the foreground. Postcard published by H.J. White of Kingswood, and posted in January 1926.

38. Another aerial view looking in the same direction towards Cossham Hospital, the tower of the hospital can just be seen on the skyline.

39. Holy Trinity Church situated in the High Street was designed by Foster and Son, their design quite plain with a square tower and a clock. The church was consecrated and dedicated in September 1821.

40. High Street. This winter scene enables a view of the Church through the trees surrounding the Church, with shops and properties in the direction of the centre of Kingswood.

41. Kingswood Park opened in 1934. It was laid out on land adjoining Kingswood Church, a glimpse of the Church can be seen through the trees.

42. The bandstand in the park in the 1950s. This view through the archway shows a little of the attractive layout of the park.

43. Hanham Road with Moravian Road off to the left. The cottages on the right are much the same today, but the single cottage on the corner with Moravian Road has been removed for road widening, and the land developed for industrial use. The sign on the old cottage reads "Breaks, Wagonettes, Landaus, Traps to let or hire". This postcard was posted in January 1907.

44. Girl Guides and competitors in fancy dress, with decorated bicycles. The event on the placard reads "Mrs. Pankhurst's Y.M.C.A. Carnival". Picture taken by Plucknett, no doubt to raise funds for the suffragette cause.

KINGSWOOD

Kingswood·Reformatory,
John Wesley's Chapel.

45. Pictured here is the Wesleyan Chapel, with boys standing outside who attended the Kingswood Reformatory School, a day school founded by John Wesley in 1748. They were mostly sons of colliers. Later Wesley included daughters, and a boarding school for orphans, as well as an adult school.

Kingswood Reformatory, Shewing Wesley Tree.

46. In 1832 a boarding institution was founded within the reformatory, to teach the sons of Methodist Ministers, the word of Methodism. The schools were situated in Britannia Road, and this is a Boys Technical School today.

47. Cossham Memorial Hospital situated on the highest ground in Bristol, on Lodge Hill. It was built in 1907, with money bequeathed by Handel Cossham. He was a wealthy man, owning many coal mines in Kingswood and District, and for a time he was a Member of Parliament, but he never forgot the sick and underprivileged.

48. Taken in the grounds of Cossham Hospital with the Lodge at the entrance, showing soldiers convalescing from their injuries received while fighting at the front in the 1914-18 war. Like many Bristol hospitals it was used as a war hospital. The building in the distance is Kingswood Castle.

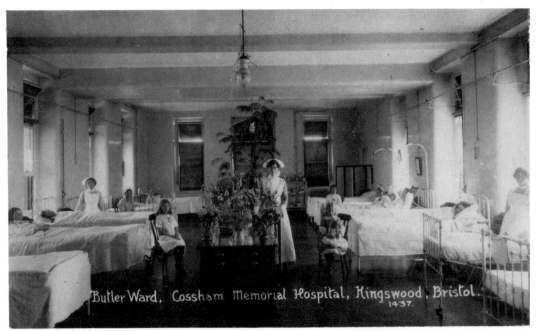

Butler Ward, Cossham Memorial Hospital, Kingswood, Bristol. 1437.

49. Butler Ward with patients, mostly children. The windows are shaded from the bright sunlight at the far end. This view is taken about 1916.

Fussell Ward, Cossham Memorial Hospital, Kingswood, Bristol. 1438

50. Fussell Ward, named after the Fussell family who owned one of the largest boot and shoe factories in Kingswood. This ward shows soldiers recovering from their injuries in the 1914-18 war.

Kingswood Castle.

51. Kingswood Castle. Although called a castle it was never a 'Castle', but an extension of a former windmill. This view shows the extensive gardens and an elaborate wooden porch, in about 1910.

The Castle, Kingswood Bristol. 370

52. This view of the 'Castle' shows clearly the round tower that was once the former windmill. The 'Castle' was situated off of Lodge Hill, quite near to Cossham Memorial Hospital as illustration 48 shows.

53. Two coaches ready for an annual Sunday School outing from Zion Chapel, parked here in Grantham Road. The second coaches registration number is HT 3734. Photograph taken by Plucknett.

54. Another outing, this one starting in London Street. The driver, standing in his white coat and cap, the coaches registration number is HT 3729. On the left the garage with many petrol signs advertised was owned by a Mr. Amos, whose grandfather Alfred Amos built the Memorial Clock Tower in Regent Street. Another Plucknett photo.

55. Pratts Boot Factory in Park Road, one of the many boot and shoe manufacturers in the Kingswood area, this factory is now demolished.

56. Kingswood Fire Brigade. The crew with their driver, Harry Bamford, who came from a well-known Kingswood family.

57. High Street showing the varied selection of shops from the lower end of Kingswood, a Bristol Co-operative Society sign by the horse and cart. The postcard was postally used in 1912.

58. Further down the High Street from illustration 57, a Midland Railway cart can be seen near the wall of the Church. This photo was taken in the early 1900s and sent as a Christmas Greeting card.

59. Looking down the High Street with a small girl standing by the entrance to Holy Trinity Church. The long shadows of the trees add to the interest of this view. Postcard published by York, before 1914.

60. Another view in the opposite direction from illustration number 59. Photo taken by Hepworth in early 1926.

61. Kingswood School on the left opened in 1892. The tower of Kingswood Parish Church can be seen in the centre distance. The premises on the right are on the corner of Alma Road in this photograph taken about 1910.

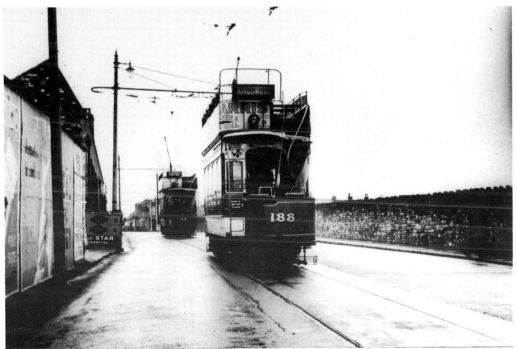

62. Further down the High Street towards Warmley, trams no.33 and 188 approaching the tram depot in Hill Street in the 1930s.

63. Looking in the opposite direction to illustration 61, the School prominent on the right is known as the Park School today. This view from about 1914.

64. The rear view of Fairview House, in Kingswood Hill. This house was owned by Mr. Abraham Fussell, who was in business in the shoe trade, in Warmley, in Old Market Street, and Lawrence Hill. The house is now Fairview Nursing Home at 42, Hill Street. The postcard was posted from Fairview House to Horfield, Bristol in November 1907.

65. Hill St., also known as Kingswood Hill in about 1910, looking down the hill in the direction of Warmley, with a variation of architecture in the terraced houses and the three storey shops.

66. Taken at the bottom of Kingswood Hill, as it levels out into Deanery Road and Warmley Village.

67. Mr. & Mrs. Arthur Tanner and family outside Holly Cottage, in Deanery Road, Warmley, taken in 1912. Mr. Tanner was the local insurance agent, and the cottage is still in existence today near the Tennis Court Inn.

68. Deanery Road. The house middle left is the same one as that on the right of illustration 66. Next door to the Hardware Stores on the right is a petrol pump advertising B.P. Petrol at 1/5d (7½p) and for commercial users 1/4 (7p) a gallon!

69. High Street, Warmley, which continues into Deanery Road. The Station Hotel on the left was serving Georges Beers, with Sidney Fussell's coal yard on the right of the picture in the early 1920s.

70. The War Memorial newly erected in the small park in Warmley, about 1920. An artillery gun, a relic of the First World War, is on display.

71. Warmley Station. A distant view of the railway track near Warmley Station, with a steam train in the station and many coal wagons in the sidings, serving the coal mines in the surrounding area. This picture was taken in 1906.

72. Warmley Station was opened in 1869 on the Midlands' New Mangotsfield to Bath branch line. It was closed to goods traffic in 1965, and passengers in 1966.

73. Warmley Harvest Festival. This picture was taken outside the Midland Railway Hotel in the early 1920s.

74. Fussell's coal yard opposite the Station Hotel showing a traction engine attached to an empty coal wagon. The coal yard workers have stopped work for the photographer in this early picture. The Station Hotel is selling Ashton Gate Beers, in later years it sold Georges Beers, as in illustration 69.

75. William T. Jefferies, grocer of Warmley, states the nameboard on the open cart. The man is in working clothes and the woman is wearing a mans cap. An advert on the wall of the building is advertising Spratts Patent Puppy Biscuits.

76. Mr. W.T. Jefferies, Baker and Grocer, their delivery horse and cart with the driver and assistant. The large baskets hanging on the front of the cart were for carrying bread.

77. The Parish Church of Warmley, St. Barnabas, with the vicarage and Schools adjoining and fields opposite, in 1907.

78. The same view in the early 1920s. Church Avenue now has semi-detached houses built on the field.

79. A close view of St. Barnabas Church, showing the Church in its rural setting, and its distinctive spire.

80. The vicarage of St. Barnabas, with the altar window of the Church just visible through the trees.

81. William Jefferies, Grocer and Baker, of Stanley Road. Their horse-drawn delivery cart parked outside the stable, next door to their shop. Photograph taken about 1910.

82. A close-up view of the Jefferies family, with the families horse and trap outside their shop in 1915. The horse's name was Topper.

83. Mr. G.A. Tanner's left hand drive delivery van, a model T. Ford registration number XE 3162, with the driver Mr. Fred Gay. Their delivery area included Syston Common and Cadbury Heath as well as Warmley.

84. Tower Road before 1910. The Post Office is on the right behind the two men. An advertisement for Brooks Dye Works, and a notice for the public telephone call office, one of the early services at the time, can be seen above their heads.

KINGSWOOD INDEX

WARMLEY INDEX